THE "IN" DISEASE OF THE NINETIES

From word processor operators to factory chicken pluckers, our in-
dustrialized society has spawned millions of jobs whose hallmark is
a consistent repetitive motion involving the wrist and arm. This
relentless stress combined with a sedentary lifestyle and sub-optimal
diet has resulted in a dysfunction of epidemic proportions: carpal
tunnel syndrome (CTS).

This informative handbook outlines the causes and symptoms of
CTS, the tests that can diagnose it, and, most important, a host of
nonsurgical treatment options from workplace adjustments to physical and neuromuscular therapy, acupuncture and reflexology, nutrition and vitamin supplementation.

ABOUT THE AUTHOR

Ray C. Wunderlich, Jr. received his M.D. from Columbia University. He is board-certified by the American Academy of Pediatrics and the American College for the Advancement of Medicine, and practices preventive medicine and health promotion in St. Petersburg, Florida. He is the author of many books on nutrition and health including *Sugar and Your Health; Kids, Brains, and Learning;* and *Help for New Parents and Parents-To-Be*. Dr. Wunderlich is also co-author, with Dwight Kalita, of another Good Health Guide, *Candida Albicans*, also published by Keats Publishing.

The Natural Treatment of Carpel Tunnel Syndrome

How to treat "computer wrist" without surgery

Ray C. Wunderlich, Jr., M.D.

Keats Publishing, Inc.  New Canaan, Connecticut

NOTICE

For simplicity throughout this text I shall use the masculine pronoun when in actuality I intend the meaning to include both males and females. No gender bias is intended.

CONTENTS

ACKNOWLEDGMENTS

I wish to acknowledge the assistance of many persons who supplied me with information for this text. Many of these special persons I have referred to directly in the text. Others not mentioned in the text but often equally important are: Edie Cox, Access Imaging (Magnetic Imaging Center); Jon Pangborn, Ph.D., President, Bionostics, Inc.; Royce Hobby, M.D.; Eduardo Raheb, M.D.; and Joanne Gessler, B.M.

I also want to thank the dedicated members of my office staff: Elinor Wunderlich, R.N., Kierstine Bayle, L.P.N., Sarah Weeks, Martha Schales, B.S., Charlotte Romine, Dick Van Middlesworth, R.N., Maria Schulke, L.M.T., and Ann Bozeman, accountant and typist.

Ray C. Wunderlich, Jr., M.D.
St. Petersburg, Florida

INTRODUCTION

The carpal tunnel syndrome (CTS) is an annoying condition in which pain and peculiar sensations in the fingers, hands, wrists, and arms may lead to impairment of hand function. The condition may involve either one or both sides, but it is more often bilateral than unilateral. The dominant hand is most often affected. Women of middle age are most susceptible. If not appropriately treated, CTS may eventuate in permanent nerve and muscle damage, but most cases can be successfully managed with complete recovery. In our society, CTS has become a common disorder.

I wish to state at the outset that I recognize the need for surgery in the management of CTS in some patients. Rarely, however, is surgery needed for this condition as an emergency. Therefore, a considerable period of time exists for most patients to explore and utilize natural therapies, if they choose to do so.

As far as conventional *medical* management of the condition is concerned, the care consists of one of six options: 1) referral to a surgeon; 2) referral to a physical therapist or neuromuscular therapist; 3) treatment with pharmacological agents such as the non-steroidal anti-inflammatory drugs and/or diuretics; 4) treatment of certain diseases or conditions that underlie CTS and serve as precipitants for the disorder; 5) intercession for alteration of the patient's job; or 6) utilization of some of the natural approaches that are to be covered in this text.

The medical conditions that might underlie CTS include pregnancy, premenstrual syndrome, use of birth control pills, hypothyroidism, and diabetes mellitus. (Those states may give rise to CTS by virtue of fluid retention and possible relative or absolute nutrient deficits.) Other possible underlying medical disorders are sarcoidosis, rheumatoid arthritis, osteoarthritis, gout, acromegaly, amyloidosis, tumors, Paget's disease of bone, fractures, and dislocations. These latter conditions, although possibly involving fluid retention and relative or absolute nutrient deficits, are more likely to induce CTS by more direct mechanical factors. In order to appreciate the manner in which mechanical factors contribute to the origin of CTS, we must now examine, to some degree, the structure of the wrist.

ANATOMY

In medical terms the wrist is known as the carpus. A prominent feature of the wrist is the carpal tunnel, a space through which the nine tendons of the forearm muscles and the median nerve course to the hand. The tunnel is formed by a stout band of connective tissue, the transverse carpal ligament, that is also known as the transverse metacarpal ligament, and the flexor retinaculum.[1] That stout ligament spans across the concave bony arch formed by the eight wrist (carpal) bones (See Figure 1).

According to Caillet the tunnel extends from the wrist into the hand for a distance of three centimeters (1.18 inches).[2] For that reason (although we customarily think of the carpal tunnel as being situated *at* the wrist), we understand that the carpal tunnel is actually situated at the most shoulderward (proximal) part of the hand. Caillet states: "This tunnel would be deep enough to permit the entrance of a finger if all its contents were removed."[1] In addition to the tendons of the flexor muscles (that insert upon the bones of the hand and fingers) and their sheaths, the tunnel contains blood vessels as well as the median nerve.

Anyone who has driven in a tunnel recognizes that it, by definition, is a limited space in which there can be a great deal of traffic. There is little or no extra space. In *this* tunnel, the carpal tunnel, the lines of "traffic" (the flexor tendons, blood vessels, and median nerve) lie side by side very close to one another.

Some tunnels may be constitutionally different from others'. Crouch and Madden, in their fine booklet on CTS, discuss the "square" wrist, an anatomical configuration that appears to predispose one to CTS.[3] They indicate that one can use calipers to measure the height and width of the wrist at the wrist crease closest to the

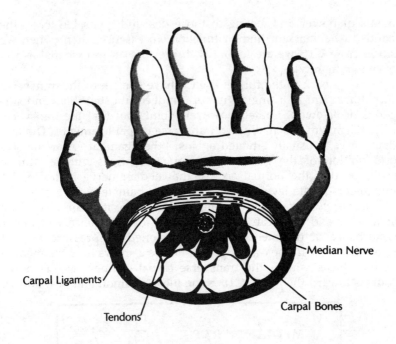

Carpal Ligaments

Tendons

Median Nerve

Carpal Bones

Figure 1. Diagrammatic sketch of the carpal tunnel and its contents. (From *Living with C.T.D.* by Lauren A. Hebert, PT, IMPACC, Bangor, Maine. Used with permission of the publisher.)

palm. Then divide the thickness by the width. A "square" wrist is said to be present when the ratio is .7 or higher. Small-sized wrists also appear to predispose to CTS.

In the process of evolution, man's forelimbs were freed from locomotion and became the prehensile hands that I use today to write these very words. The stout ligament across the wrist that forms the carpal tunnel may have had a protective function when we were quadrupedal (if one wishes to think in evolutionary terms). We know, however, that humans suffer no disabilities at all when the ligament is cut through (for relief of CTS). Hence, the stout transverse carpal ligament may be viewed as an anatomical vestige of our past.

The human hand with its power grip, its precise, pincer grip, and its unique sensory capacities depends for its integrity upon the carpal tunnel and its ability to successfully channel the anatomical elements of power and feeling to those near-indispensable tools, the hands, a hallmark of human function. In essence, then, when we suffer from CTS we are toying with the loss of an essential aspect of our humanity.

But now back to the tunnel itself. I have spoken of the transverse carpal ligament as a single structure. Indeed, most authors and surgeons do likewise. Caillet, however, points out that the transverse carpal ligament is actually two transverse carpal ligaments. The median nerve is usually situated against "the ligament" near the second tendon of the flexor digitorum superficialis muscle. Runge indicates that the normal size of the median nerve is 4.5 by 2.1 millimeters at the level of the hook of the hamate wrist bone.[4]

The *sine qua non* of CTS is compression of the median nerve. The symptoms and signs can all be accounted for by a sensory or motor disturbance of the median nerve occasioned by pressure exerted upon the nerve in the carpal tunnel. Figure 2 shows how the median nerve "ducks" under the transverse carpal ligament as the nerve courses toward the hand. CTS is the most common and best known

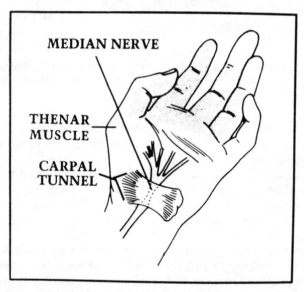

Figure 2. Graphic sketch of the median nerve coursing under the transverse carpal ligament of the wrist. (From the newsletter of the Florida Chapter of the Arthritis Foundation, March, 1992, Vol. XX, No. 1. Used with the permission of the Arthritis Foundation.)

example of an entrapment neuropathy in which a nerve is compromised in function as a result of surrounding anatomical tissues.

According to the strictly anatomical view of CTS, the symptoms and signs of median-nerve dysfunction occur in a characteristic distribution that includes the palm (especially the thumb-side of the palm), the first three fingers, and often the thumb-side or radial side of the ring finger. Disturbance of the sensory aspect of the median nerve gives rise to diminished touch sensation (numbness), diminished perception of pain, or paresthesias (tingling, burning, pins and needles sensation) in the location described. Disturbance of the motor aspect of the median nerve gives rise to weakness of grip between the thumb, index, and middle fingers (weakened pincer grasp or opposition of thumb to index finger), faulty flexion of the first three fingers (especially the index finger), and atrophy of the muscles at the base of the thumb on the palmar side (the thenar muscles). The sensory symptoms usually dominate the early clinical picture. Weakness of the abductor pollicis brevis, a thumb muscle that pulls the thumb outward away from the index finger, is a sign of median nerve dysfunction.

Although the median nerve distribution usually occurs as described, anatomical variations do happen. For example, the entire hand may be innervated by the median nerve or by the ulnar nerve. Electrical diagnosis by means of electromyography with nerve conduction testing may identify such variations and provide evidence for entrapment neuropathy.

SYMPTOMS

What leads the individual with CTS to seek assistance for his condition? The presenting symptoms and signs are rather characteristic. Usual complaints are pain in the wrist, hand, or fingers; however, discomfort in the forearm may also be present. Paresthesias such as numbness (falling asleep), tingling, pins and needles sensations, burning, and itching are common. Swelling of the hands and fingers may occur but often the feeling of swelling is reported when no edema can be seen.

Clumsiness, weak grip, or dropping objects may also be noted. Difficulty in grasping, pinching, opening jars, or buttoning and un-buttoning may occur. There may be morning stiffness of the fingers, swollen feeling in the hands or fingers, impaired finger flexions, and transient night-time paralysis of the hand. Testing by touching with a cotton wisp or by light pin-prick may disclose diminished sensation. Caillet has emphasized the nocturnal nature of the pares-thesias and numbness.[1] Although some authors indicate that flexion of the wrist will aggravate symptoms, Caillet indicates the opposite: that extension (dorsiflexion or elevation of the hand in relation to the wrist) is an aggravating factor (when coupled with gripping or flexion of the fingers). Caillet also reports that CTS patients will experience tingling and numbness in the fingers when a blood-pres-sure cuff is inflated around the arm. Undoubtedly that procedure increases the pressure in the carpal tunnel and thus also the pres-sure on the median nerve.

THE ELLIS FUNCTIONAL TEST

A test to identify the presence of CTS was presented by Dr. John Ellis (as noted in Werbach's description[1]). The Ellis Test is a test of disordered function of the hand(s). It goes like this:

1. Hold the hands out with palms up.
2. Bend the fingers at the two outer joints only leaving the joints which join the fingers to the palm in a straight line with the wrist.
3. Bring the tips of the fingers down to the palms of the hands right to the crease that separates the fingers from the hands.
4. If any of these 16 joints cannot be bent completely and without pain, carpal tunnel syndrome is suspect.

I have found the Ellis Test to be a sensitive indicator of disturbed function of the hand(s). However, in my experience, the test can also be abnormal in the presence of osteoarthritis or rheumatoid arthritis as well as serving as an indicator of CTS.

CAUSATIVE FACTORS

Possible causes of CTS (median-nerve compression) include scarring, thickening or swelling of the transverse carpal ligament, the tendons and/or their sheaths, the blood vessels and/or the connective tissue around them, and loose connective tissue in the tunnel. In addition, thickening of the nerve itself must be considered. Caillet makes the statement that approximately 50 percent of the nerve is connective tissue.[1] Hence there is reason to believe that thickening of the nerve itself might be one cause of CTS.

CTS occurs rather frequently in pregnancy, hence it is not surprising that the condition is encountered also in patients who habitually take the birth control pill which operates by inducing a state of "mini-pregnancy." Patients with underactive thyroid function commonly are edematous. In fact, the classical hypothyroid state is known as myxedema. The increased frequency of CTS in hypothyroid individuals may well be associated with their tendency to collect unwanted fluid in body tissues. Remember, the carpal tunnel is a crowded tunnel. Fluid collection from the hormones of pregnancy, birth control pills, or hypothyroidism may swell the tissues and compress the median nerve.

Patients with diabetes mellitus do not escape the tendency to collect fluid to an abnormal degree. We remember that sugar is an osmotically active substance. Thus it holds water until it is metabolized away. Diabetics may have other reasons for their propensity for CTS, but undue fluid retention likely is one.

Those persons who ingest much salt and/or sugar, especially those who are physically inactive, may also swell inordinately and thus predispose themselves to CTS. I suspect, too, that the proclivity for swelling in the premenstrual phase of women's menstrual cycles accounts for the definite tendency of some women to have CTS in the second half of their cycles.

One of the most common causes of swelling, often cryptic in origin because it may not even be considered as a possible cause of swelling, is allergic edema. Of all the allergic causes, reactions to foods are the most prevalent in my experience. Thus the individual with CTS may have any or all of the prior conditions (or none of the prior conditions) as well as food allergies.

Certain conditions such as rheumatoid arthritis, osteoarthritis, gout, injury, cysts, tumors, and the like may give rise to compression of the median nerve. Rheumatoid arthritis is more often causative of CTS than other forms of arthritis because of the extensive proliferation of the synovial lining of the joints in that illness. Other disorders associated with CTS are acromegaly (a rare disease of the pituitary gland but very often associated with CTS), sarcoidosis, and amyloidosis.

A most dramatic case of CTS came to me recently. An 84-year-old woman had an abrupt onset of pain, numbness, tingling, and inability to use the thumb, index, and middle fingers of the dominant hand. She questioned a stroke. The involved hand was swollen in the described areas. History taking revealed that a few days earlier she had started taking a diuretic type of antihypertensive drug. There was a strong family history of gout. Laboratory tests revealed an elevation of uric acid, the "gout chemical." Elimination of the diuretic drug and treatment of the gout was promptly followed by disappearance of all symptoms. In that case, CTS due to gouty arthritis of the wrist and hand had apparently been precipitated by use of the diuretic drug.

REPETITIVE MOVEMENTS

The prolonged repetitive movements involved in certain occupations or hobbies may also be a cause of CTS. But if that is indeed the case, why then do not all persons engaged in such movements develop CTS? The answer is that each one of us is different, with different support factors, and a different set of additional stressors that impinge upon us to interfere with our ability to withstand the local microtraumas of repetitive movements.

CTS must be considered a risk factor in the following occupations or activities: jackhammer workers, computer keyboard operators, assembly line workers, carpenters, supermarket checkers, ditch diggers, needleworkers and knitters, gymnasts, racquet-ball players, secretaries, typists, horse groomers, hairdressers, waiters, sign-language interpreters, cashiers, factory and farm workers, mechanics, surgeons, butchers, tennis players, musicians, and others. One patient in my practice is a confectioner. The repetitive movements involved in making cotton candy and candied apples hour after hour precipitated her bilateral CTS. Significantly, she is also hypothyroid. The common denominator in all these occupations or activities—as well as in others that I have not mentioned—is the use and overuse of the wrist at work or play.

Let us consider CTS in musicians. Because musical instruments involve the use of the hands, CTS is a definite risk. Although any musician may develop CTS, most commonly pianists are affected. String players are the next most likely to be involved.

According to Hunter Fry, M.D., an Australian plastic surgeon, 64 percent of musicians in professional orchestras have painful overuse syndromes of their lips, hands, thumbs, etc.[2] Any musician—pop, rock, country, or jazz—is vulnerable to injury. Those most affected perform repetitive movements for long hours. The common diagnosis is tendinitis from overuse.

As Richard Lederman, M.D. pointed out, the overuse may seem to produce symptoms as the result of a single event, but usually an accumulation of milder stresses over time is responsible for the pain and hand/arm dysfunction.[3] Dr. Lederman noted that keyboard instrumentalists have more problems with the right hand and arm whereas the bowed-string instrumentalists such as violin and viola players usually manifest left hand and arm problems.

In the case of pianists, "banging the keys" for six to eight hours every day often exceeds the capacity of the tissues to remain healthy. Ignace Jan Paderewski had a right-hand disorder attributed to the rigors of his piano concert schedule. Pianist-composer Robert Schumann was known to have a serious affliction of the right hand that eventually forced him to stop playing the piano. He fashioned a kind of a splint that he used. Today many pianists with CTS must use a splint to immobilize the wrist when they are not playing.

Concert pianists Gary Graffman and Leon Fleischer were among the first of their profession to publicly acknowledge that they suffered from music-related disorders. Both eventually made comebacks, but only after lengthy sabbaticals. Fleisher resumed his career after successful surgery on his right wrist 17 years after his initial difficulties.

The most common complaints of pianists are: loss of control, speed, and facility in playing trills, arpeggios, and octaves; loss of endurance; and a feeling of weakness in the hand. The right hand is involved more than the left. Many performers, believing that their symptoms stem from technical or artistic errors, push themselves to longer practice periods, thus aggravating their CTS.

Right-handed pianists who have CTS and other disorders of the dominant hand have available a body of works composed specifically for the left hand. Much of this stems from Paul Wittgenstein, who commissioned pieces from composers after he lost his right arm in World War I.

The question arises as to what movements of the wrist are most apt to induce CTS. Repetitive flexion of the hand on the wrist is, indeed, quite likely a cause because the known physiology of muscles explains thickening of tendons as the result of repetitive muscle flexion. Davis' Law states that contraction of a muscle increases the thickness of the muscle and its tendons.[4] Hence, repetitive flexion movements of the forearm muscles can thicken those muscles as well as their tendons to crowd the median nerve in the carpal tunnel and thus to produce compression neuropathy.

The origin of CTS in cases of sustained or repetitive extension of the hand or the wrist is perhaps more difficult to fathom. One postulates that the extended posture induces a diminution in blood supply to the median nerve. It appears that repetitive motion overuse of the hands, whether it be with flexion, extension, or even twisting is associated with CTS. Caillet pointed out that increased pressure in the carpal tunnel has been found with both flexion and extension.[5]

WRIST POSITION AND POSTURE

Certainly wrist position must be considered a factor of origin as are trauma, pounding, body position to wrists and hands, nutritive status, glandular function, overall health, etc. The mechanical factors seem most likely to be primary precipitants of CTS. However, I stress again that the make-up of the individual—the nature of his tissues—during the time of the repetitive-motion activities must also be considered as a most significant permissive factor for the development of CTS.

Lauren Hebert, a physical therapist, has emphasized the following risk factors for CTS:
1. Bending wrist forward (flexion),
2. Tipping wrist toward little finger (deviation),

3. Turning palm up into supination,
4. Grip (wide, forceful, prolonged),
5. Pinch (repeated, prolonged, or forceful),
6. Excessive thumb work, and
7. Cold, vibration, direct pressure to wrist.[6]

Sustained posture may be a vital component of the CTS. Holding the body upright throughout a work day can be most taxing. Moreover, the head, the weight of a bowling ball, must be held firmly in order that the eyes can fixate on what the hands are about. Commonly the head is permitted to fall forward instead of being held upright in line with the spine. The forward position of the head contributes additional stress on the neck, shoulders, and trunk. It may also alter the position of the jaws, resulting in temperomandibular joint dysfunction (TMJ disorder).

As Hebert points out, CTS is an example of a disorder in which there are few if any outward manifestations of the condition until very late in the disorder when muscular atrophy may be apparent.[6] He calls it an "invisible" disorder. However, electrical nerve conduction studies or magnetic resonance imaging of the wrist(s) may provide the objective evidence needed to verify the diagnosis.

STRESS

No text on a specific disorder such as CTS would be complete without a discussion of that most prevalent general factor—stress. By stress I mean *dys*-stress, the state of harassment that results when one is unhappy, unfulfilled, worried, uncertain, overburdened, fearful, guilty, underexercised, underrested, and generally malcontent. Sometimes *dys*-stress is evident at a conscious level, but many times it may be present and unknown to its owner. If, for example, one has moved his residence, lost a loved one, or has been threatened with a lawsuit, he may be unaware that he is stressed, but the likelihood is great that he is.

Stress (*dys*-stress) leads to tight muscles, and tight muscles are accompanied by a relative lack of blood supply and inordinate build-up of waste metabolic products such as lactic acid in tissues. Stress also may rob the body of nutrients or increase the metabolic demand therefore. In fact, many of the deleterious effects of classic stress may owe their origin to the nutrient deficits rather than the more direct effects of stress itself upon the systems of the body. My clinical experience supports the observation that many individuals escape unscathed from states of classic stress when their nutrient needs are optimally met.

Lauren Hebert, writing about stress, states: "The body works harder and tolerates it less!"[6] The individual with CTS who operates with the burden of chronic stress may unknowingly dig himself into a deeper pit of dysfunction when a local disorder such as CTS fails to respond to therapies that might otherwise clear it rather promptly. In other words, the pressure of classic stress can only have a negative effect upon any localized disorder such as CTS, and the CTS itself adds to the individual's stress burden.

OTHER CAUSES OF CTS

Many orthopedic surgeons routinely obtain an X-ray of the wrist(s) when they suspect CTS in order to identify the disorders that can cause CTS. Dislocation or fracture of the carpal bones may be the cause as well as tumors, arthritic spurs, ganglia or other cysts. One must also be aware that carpal tunnel compression is not the only cause of median nerve dysfunction. A condition known as neuritis or nerve inflammation may also be the culprit.

CTS AS REPAIR DEFICIT

Russell Jaffe, M.D., Ph.D. (Director, Seramune Physician's Laboratory, Reston, Va.) sees CTS as a repair deficit. Jaffe holds the view, in essence, that the body's machinery and store of raw materials and operative "know how" for maintenance and repair have been switched off, or they are unavailable because of more vital functions in which they are engaged. Jaffe sees the body's repair resources, in other words, as limited and sometimes not available because of needed work ongoing in other projects of a higher priority to the body's overall economy.

In a repair deficit, connective tissue, traumatized by repetitive movements or other assaults upon its integrity, fails to properly rebuild or repair itself to a normal, nonpainful state. In CTS, the connective tissues in need of repair may be the antebrachial fascia, the transverse carpal ligament or flexor retinaculum, the nine flexor tendons in the carpal tunnel (Figure 1), and the connective tissues that serve as the sheaths of the tendons and the median nerve.

Failure to repair could be due to inadequate raw materials needed for the repair (Vitamin C, glucosamine, amino acids, manganese, chondroitin sulfate, etc.), the continuation of a state of assault upon the various connective tissues in and around the carpal tunnel, or the unavailability of the repair process for the local carpal tissue repair. All three of these factors may be fostered by certain adverse conditions that may become established in the body. A depleted "warehouse" of raw materials for repair, a continuing assault upon the tissues of the wrist already sensitized (traumatized) by repetitive movements, and a diversion of the repair process of the body's anabolic mechanism are produced or intensified by the following states:

1. faulty bowel flora (intestinal dysbiosis),
2. intestinal parasites,
3. intestinal Candida-yeast overgrowth,
4. faulty digestion and/or absorption of foods,
5. "leaky" (hyperpermeable) gut,
6. undernourishment as a result of faulty diet,
7. adverse reactions to foods and chemicals,
8. toxic body burdens.

Undoubtedly, there are other states that also qualify as detractors or diverters of the repair process. Stress, for example, has already been discussed.

CTS AS VITAMIN B6 DEFICIENCY

Perhaps the most prominent nutrient deficiency linked with almost all cases of CTS is vitamin B6 (pyridoxal-5-phosphate). The medical literature is full of research illustrating the frequent clinical success obtained in treatment of CTS with B6.

Biochemical evidence of vitamin B6 status in the body is provided by measurement of an enzyme in red blood cells (erythrocytes) called glutamic-oxaloacetic transaminase (EGOT). Whenever B6 is low, the functional activity of EGOT is low.

Ellis et al. in 1976 studied ten patients with CTS.[1] They found abnormally low activity level of EGOT indicating inadequacy of B6. The patients improved with B6 supplementation. In a follow-up study in 1977, 11 additional patients with CTS were also found deficient in B6 by assay of the EGOT enzyme.[2] These patients also responded nicely to treatment with B6.

In 1978, Folkers, Ellis, et al. studied a single patient with CTS.[3] The patient was found to have a low level of EGOT. He improved when given 2 mg of B6 per day but improved even more when 100 mg per day were given. The improvement was clinical as well as biochemical. After being placed on placebo therapy, his clinical symptoms returned and the EGOT activity deteriorated. Reinstitution of B6 at 100 mg per day was followed by disappearance of symptoms again and correction again of the low EGOT activity.

The efficiency of B6 in the treatment of CTS was established by John Ellis, M.D., in a landmark double blind study in 1982.[4] In 1984, further evidence of the beneficial effect of B6 in CTS was reported in the medical literature.[5] Beyers et al., however, suggested that the beneficial effect of B6 may be related to the presence of an unrecognized peripheral neuropathy, that is, a primary disorder of the nerve itself rather than the carpal tunnel.[6]

In 1993 Bernstein et al. found that vitamin B6 at 200 mg per day for three months dramatically improved pain scores and had no adverse effects.[7]

Dr. Russell Jaffe (see previous section: "CTS as Repair Deficit") and Jonathan Wright, M.D., as well as other physicians who practice nutritional medicine, believe that nearly every case of CTS will respond to vitamin B6 therapy; however, the dose administered may need to be extraordinarily high, perhaps as much as 3000 mg per day. Those who require extraordinary amounts of B6 in order for their EGOT cellular enzyme to function properly are said to be pyridoxine (B6) dependent. The recommended daily allowance for B6, that is, the amount required by the average individual for normal function, is 2 mg per day. Long-term use (over three years) of 200 mg or more per day has been reported to cause neurological dysfunction[8, 9] and liver injury.[10] However, the use of the active form of vitamin B6 (pyridoxal-5-phosphate) is believed to minimize or eradicate the toxicity of B6 observed with the use of the cheaper pyridoxine hydrochloride.[11] The beneficial effect of B6 should be obtained within three or four months if the dose has been proper for the individual. A trial period of three months should be utilized before judging the effectiveness or failure of B6.

Russell Jaffe, M.D., Ph.D. points out that not all commercially available preparations labeled as pyridoxal-5-phosphate actually contain that substance. Rather, they may merely contain a mixture of pyridoxine hydrochloride and some form of phosphate.

Special attention to vitamin B6 status must be directed to patients who are taking certain medications that interfere with vitamin B6 nutriture. Those medications are birth control pills, some antibiotics, isoniazid (antituberculosis), tranylcypromine (antidepressants), amphetamines (stimulants), and hydralazine and reserpine (both antihypertensives). I personally suspect that caffeine, if carefully tested, would prove to be a B6 antagonist.

Carl Folkers, Ph.D., D.Sc., M.D. (honorary) indicates that CTS is almost a specifically B6-responsive disorder.[12] He states that other nutrients are important in supporting the B6 (for example, vitamin B2). Dr. Folkers recommends 100 to 400 mg of "ordinary" B6 (pyridoxine hydrochloride) per day. Response is expected within three to four months. Dr. Folkers' advice to the patients is to continue the B6 "as long as you eat." In regard to the problem of B6 toxicity, he indicates that significant toxicity is only seen in doses of the order of three grams per day over long periods.

In patients with CTS, blood levels of vitamin B6 are rarely helpful in management. The levels are usually found to be normal, and the levels give no indication of the functional efficacy of the EGOT enzyme. Although the generally effective therapeutic dose for CTS is 100 to 200 mg per day, enormous doses may be required in some individuals.

Hugh Riordan, M.D. and Marvin Dirks, B.D., M.A. of the Center for Improvement of Human Functioning in Wichita, Kan., recently attempted to study CTS and B6 via enzyme measurements in a small group of patients who were surgical failures. Their conclusion was that there are, indeed, many factors to be taken into account that are probably just as important as B6 supplementation. Those factors may be diet, lifestyle, digestion and absorption, medications, prior surgeries, concomitant diseases, and other nutrient deficits (vitamin B2, for example), etc. I heartily concur in that view. In patients in whom there can be established an absence of zinc deficiency, an adequacy of dietary protein, a functionally competent gastrointestinal tract, a well-functioning biochemical metabolism, an unencumbered lifestyle and psychosocial adjustment, B6 may prove to be a single factor of importance in the development of CTS and its treatment. Nearly always, however, a multiplicity of issues must be probed, confronted, and managed if one is to ensure the health of the wrist along with general health in the rest of the body.

FUNCTIONAL ENZYME TEST OF B6

The EGOT reaction, as has been noted, is a cardinal test for B6 status in the body. A single blood test may prove to be abnormal indicating that the amount of vitamin B6 obtained from the patient's diet or from supplements is inadequate for the needs of metabolism. In order to find the dose of oral B6 that will normalize the functional assay, a series of EGOT tests can be performed as the dose of B6 given to the patient is increased. The endpoint and the recommended final dose of B6 is that amount of B6 that produces no further improvement in the EGOT test.

Jonathan Wright, M.D., has described a patient investigated and treated by such testing.[1] In earlier years Folkers, Ellis *et al.* had shown in a patient with severe CTS and a low EGOT that progressive improvement in the EGOT followed successive increases in the dose of B6 from 2 mg to 100 mg per day.[2] Moreover, cessation of B6 treatment was accompanied by a return of the abnormally low EGOT and worsening of clinical symptoms. The patient became asymptomatic and the EGOT became normal upon resumption of B6 supplementation at 100 mg per day.

When one reflects on the common clinical use of B6 as a natural diuretic, particularly to combat fluid retention in the premenstrual state, its use to decongest swollen tissues in the wrist makes sense. Perhaps the clinical effectiveness of B6 in CTS is unrelated to that diuretic action or, more likely, there are two effects: one, an improvement of tissue metabolism, and two, (perhaps a consequence of the first) a reduction in swelling.

From the assembled evidence that I have cited in this text, one is led to believe that vitamin B6 is a most consistently effective natural treatment for CTS. Lest I be considered biased or an advocate of closed thought, however, I call the reader's attention to the paper of Smith et al.[3] These authors studied six patients with CTS who were treated with B6 (100 mg daily for nine to 26 weeks). In all cases, enzyme function and B6 levels were normal and showed no consistent change with B6 treatment. Clinical improvement was not significant. The authors write that a large double-blind controlled trial would be necessary to show that B6 treatment is genuinely effective in CTS.

Rarely is there unanimity of opinion in regard to the treatment of medical conditions as elusive as CTS. One can argue that the burden of proof rests upon further scientific research to demonstrate that B6 has genuine value in CTS. I, for one, profess the view that B6 (along with a host of other substances) is a valuable adjunct in nutritional medicine for bringing patients to a higher plane of health and well-being. I shall continue to see B6 as the most important tool of help for patients with CTS as well as many other disorders unless more compelling evidence surfaces to indicate otherwise.

Perhaps the final word on B6 status of an individual belongs to the dean of nutritional biochemistry, Jon Pangborn, Ph.D. of Chicago. Pangborn points out that B6 status in the body can be assessed in a number of different ways, including EGOT and kynurenic/ xanthurenic acid tests.[4] Dr. Pangborn states that the quantitative assay of P-5-P is a "good" test. The collection of all urine passed in a 24-hour period permits the accurate measurement of more than 40 amino acids and peptides. Among those, at least 12 require B6 in their metabolism. Accordingly, when those 12 amino acids are elevated, the laboratory has provided strong evidence of B6 need. The specific ratio of the amino acid methionine to the amino acid cystathionine serves too as an indicator of B6 need. Normal methionine in the presence of a low level of cystathionine indicates that B6 is in short supply.

Dr. Pangborn's vast experience with clinical disorders and laboratory evaluations leads him to also suggest that vitamin E is likely to be a key agent for antioxidant protection in nerve sheaths.

PSEUDO-CARPAL TUNNEL SYNDROME

Judith Walker, L.M.T. a neuromuscular therapist and educator in St. Petersburg, Fla., has stressed that symptoms and signs of CTS may have their origin not in the wrist but in the neck, shoulder, or arm. Ms. Walker relates that therapists sometimes see patients who have had surgery on the wrist and even surgery on the shoulder or neck but still retain the symptoms of pain, numbness, burning, itching, or pins and needles in the wrist or hand. In such cases the origin of the symptoms is usually found in the muscles (or the fascial connective-tissue sheaths enveloping the muscles) of the arm above the wrist. I term such cases pseudo-carpal tunnel syndrome (pseudo-CTS).

In actuality pseudo-CTS could have its origin in a wide variety of conditions. They include: spinal-cord disease; vertebral dislocation, subluxation, or arthritic spurs with nerve impingement; intervertebral disc disease; thoracic-outlet compression (cervical rib, scalene entrapment of nerves, etc.); and formation of trigger points in muscles of the neck, chest, shoulder, upper arm, and forearm. Since the median nerve derives from the brachial plexus (see Figure 3), which, in turn, derives from the cervical portion of the spinal cord, the aforementioned disorders can readily be recognized as factors of origin in pseudo-CTS.

Most commonly encountered as mimics of true CTS are trigger points in muscles or their sheaths. Judith Walker emphasizes that any muscle of the neck, shoulder, and arm must be considered a potential source of pain, numbness, paresthesias, or dysfunction in

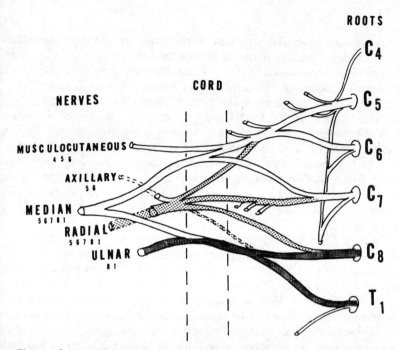

ROOTS

C_4

CORD

C_5

NERVES

C_6

MUSCULOCUTANEOUS
4 5 6

AXILLARY
5 6

C_7

MEDIAN
5 6 7 8 1

RADIAL
5 6 7 8 1

ULNAR
8 1

C_8

T_1

Figure 3. Brachial plexus (schematic) to show the origins of the median nerve from the area of the fifth cervical to the first thoracic nerve roots from the spinal cord. (From *Hand Pain and Impairment*, ed. 3, by Rene Cailliet, M.D., F. A. Davis Co., Philadelphia, 1982. Used with permission of the publisher.)

the wrist and hand. How could that be? The explanation goes like this. Muscles may become *hypertonic* (tight). The connective-tissue fascial sheaths over the muscles often become tight, wrinkled, crinkled, or otherwise dysfunctional. Tightened muscular tissues fail to be adequately perfused with blood. Think of water trying to get into a tightly squeezed sponge. That relative lack of blood supply in and out of the muscles is termed *ischemia*.

As a result of ischemia, waste products of metabolism (such as lactic acid) accumulate to form *trigger points* in the muscle. A trigger point is a tender spot identified by manual palpation that may produce symptoms of pain, tingling, numbness, burning, or pins and needles sensation at a *referred* site. A trigger point in the shoulder muscles may, for example, be responsible for symptoms in the hand. A trigger point in the subscapularis muscle classically refers to the wrist.

If and when such pseudo-CTS cases are seen by the surgeon, they must not be operated upon because more conservative measures such as deep muscle massage or neuromuscular therapy can often alleviate the condition. In the manual therapy needed (applied by a Licensed Massage Therapist, a Registered Physical Therapist or a knowledgeable physician), the trigger points are eliminated or reduced, "kinks" in the fascial connective tissue sheaths of the muscles are "ironed out," ischemia of muscle is released, proper lymph flow is restored, and the muscles are relaxed. Since muscles are the agents that pull bones (if bones are to move anywhere), one may even notice that vertebral subluxations may remit under appropriate neuromuscular therapy. For this reason, many chiropractic physicians use neuromuscular therapists as a valuable adjunct to spinal manipulation.

Paul St. John, a leading neuromuscular therapist in Largo, Florida first developed and promulgated neuromuscular therapy as it had been set forth by Raymond L. Nimmo, D.C. St. John indicates that the vast majority of CTS cases can be successfully treated by neuromuscular therapy. He, of course, refers to the identification and treatment of all causes of pseudo-CTS in the neck (scalene muscles and others), the shoulder girdle (with emphasis upon the subscapularis), the forearm muscles, as well as the tissues of the wrist(s) and hand(s). St. John emphasizes that *all* the wrist tissues—the antebrachial fascia and the flexor retinaculum (transverse carpal ligament and its attachments)—must be adequately cleared and released from hypertonus with dissolution of trigger points and "ironing out" of the connective tissues involved.

DIAGNOSIS

The foundation for proper treatment rests upon accurate diagnosis No time should be lost in carrying out a careful diagnostic assessment in patients who manifest the characteristic symptoms of CTS and the mimicking disorders. The condition belongs to no one except the individual who has it. That is to say that no one professional has exclusive rights to the diagnosis and treatment of CTS

A wide variety of professionals may be able to carry out appropriate investigation and to arrange for and supervise needed therapeutic measures. Categories that may be called upon for investigation and management could be medical physicians (orthopedists, general physicians, internists, neurologists, etc.), physical therapists, massage and neuromuscular therapists, chiropractic and osteopathic physicians, acupuncturists, radiologists, nutritionists, reflexologists, and perhaps others.

If there is any question about the diagnosis or the origin of the disorder, a physician should be consulted in order to evaluate whether there are any medical conditions present that may predispose to the disorder. Remember that CTS is encountered with inordinate frequency in persons with pregnancy, diabetes mellitus, hypothyroidism, sarcoidosis, in those on birth control pills, and in other medical conditions.

Very often the clinical picture is clear-cut, and the diagnosis of CTS can be easily made. The combination of pain, paresthesias, numbness, swelling, and interference with hand function along with nocturnal exacerbation in a person who has an occupation that requires repetitive movements for many hours at a time is classic. Of course, there are many variants to the classical picture.

The physician will perform the Tinel's test and Phalen's test. A positive Tinel's sign is the presence of tingling ("electric shock") upon tapping over the median nerve near the base of the palm and the middle of the palm. A positive Phalen's test is the production of pain, burning, numbness, tingling upon forced flexion or extension of the hand or the wrist. Increasing pressure in the forearm and wrist by use of a blood pressure cuff may also reproduce the patient's symptoms.

Nerve testing by electrical diagnosis may also be made by neurologists and sometimes by physiatrists. The electrical tests can be most helpful in establishing that median nerve dysfunction exists as well as the presence or absence of muscle dysfunction as a result. Electrical diagnosis is accurate 90 percent of the time. However, as is the case with so many tests, a normal result on the test may not absolutely exclude CTS. Most orthopedic physicians appear to utilize electrical diagnosis as an adjunct to clinical diagnosis only when the clinical picture deviates from the usual and customary presentation. Typical findings on electrical diagnosis are normal nerve velocity of conduction above the wrist with delayed nerve conduction across the ligament and into the hand and fingers.

X-rays (including CAT scans) of the wrists and sometimes the cervical spine may provide information about the presence or absence of tumors, fractures, dislocations, arthritis, arthritic spurs, cervical disc disease, etc. Magnetic resonance imaging (MRI) of the wrist may be valuable in assessing the wrist joint, the carpal tunnel, and the median nerve itself, according to Val M. Runge, M.D., a professor of diagnostic radiology at the University of Kentucky in Lexington, Ky. Dr. Runge writes: "Scar tissue, fibrosis of tendon sheaths, and tumors displacing and distorting the median nerve are easily identified with MRI." He also indicates that when the median nerve measures greater than two standard deviations above the mean, an abnormality exists.

Despite such a pronouncement, most practicing orthopedic specialists at this time see the MRI of the wrist more as a research tool than a reliable diagnostic tool. At times, MRI of the shoulder or cervical spine may be needed to elucidate rotator cuff pathology and degenerative disease of the intervertebral discs and other spinal pathologies.

As previously noted, the blood EGOT test as well as other chemical tests can provide data on the patient's need for vitamin B6.

TREATMENT

The patient with CTS is unfortunate in that he has a painful, disconcerting, and lingering condition that may threaten his occupation. He is fortunate, however, because he has a wide range of treatment options, most of which are indeed quite effective.

I have already touched on various therapies that may be utilized. Here I shall discuss additional treatments and attempt to give the reader the "flavor" of each so that he might have more information in regard to each of them.

In a nutshell, the treatments are either non-surgical or surgical. The need for surgery is not usually an urgent matter, although the patient who has not utilized one of the many noninvasive treatments is much more likely to need the knife with often a less-than-desirable outcome. Nonsurgical management includes workplace adjustment, promotion of physical fitness, nutritional measures, glandular treatment, physical therapy, neuromuscular therapy, microcurrent electrical stimulation, spinal manipulation, acupuncture, reflexology, homeopathy, and nutritional medicine.

WORKPLACE ADJUSTMENT

Needless to say, stopping the factors that produce repetitive micro-traumas of the wrist will assist greatly in improving those cases of CTS that are precipitated by repetitive movements of the hands at work. At times, the same applies to repetitive movements carried out at home, with hobbies or home activities. For those who can cease an offending occupation, that may take care of the problem. Many persons, however, are unable or unwilling to change their occupations and must be treated even though the precipitating movement factors persist.

Many times, various adjustments of work factors can be arranged. Perhaps work schedules could be adjusted so that less time is spent in the offending work mode. Often, building in stretch breaks or doing periodic loosening exercises will ease the strain of steady, demanding, repetitive movements and the demanding body postures that are necessary to support the repeated hand movements.

Diane Hartley, R.P.T. stresses that a functional analysis of the work situation must be performed.[1] At computer keyboards, a folded towel or styrofoam support under the wrists may prove helpful in positioning the hand in the neutral position. Close attention must be paid to correct seating.[2] Chairs built for tall men must be used only by tall men. The feet must be firmly planted on the floor, and the angles at the feet-ankles, lower leg-knees, and thigh-hips must all be 90 degree angles. The work station must be balanced to avoid looking only to the right or left. The arms must be freely movable.

The worker's vision must be amply corrected with lenses that permit him to sit up straight rather than lean the head forward to be closer to the object being looked at. Sometimes, simply placing books or boxes under the object to elevate it to eye level will suffice to prevent forward head.

PHYSICAL FITNESS

It may seem strange to consider the issue of physical conditioning in a discussion of the treatment of CTS, yet it is a cardinal factor in the prevention and treatment of the condition. Indeed it is no accident that persons with sedentary jobs are prominent among those who develop the disorder. Lauren Hebert, P.T. stresses the importance of physical fitness: "You must restore fitness to recover from cumulative trauma disorder, i.e., carpal tunnel syndrome, tendinitis, neck strain."[2] All aspects of fitness must be considered: strengthening, stretching, endurance, and recreation. For those who work a full work week in sedentary occupations, close attention must be given to allotted times for rest, shopping, fun, *and* programs to induce that elixir of health and healing: physical fitness. Blessed will be the day when employers foster and provide opportunities for appropriate physical conditioning at work. Blessed too will be the day when insurance companies reduce premiums for those who are physically fit.

In addition to the overall, general effect of physical conditioning on health and healing, let us not forget the therapeutic power of local exercise for the fingers, hands, arms, neck, and trunk. Stretching, toning, and strengthening the muscles (with their tendons and connective-tissue fascial coats) in those areas, when carried out in a judicious manner, can be most rewarding in building the tolerance of local tissues for the repetitive motion demands of particular occupations. Such specific exercise programs, however, must often be put on hold until acute inflammation is successfully eliminated.

NUTRITIONAL MEASURES

Hand in glove with physical fitness is nutritional well-being. The susceptible individual who develops CTS under repetitive movement micro-traumas is often nutritionally underpar. For example, a lethal combination would be a diet lacking in vegetables, a repetitive-motion occupation, and a sedentary lifestyle. Optimum nourishment, like physical fitness, can be considered an excellent buffer against stress and the development of conditions such as CTS.

The general guidelines that I suggest for eating are as follows:

1. Eat whole, fresh foods as much as possible rather than refined, packaged foods.
2. Eat a broad diet that includes as many foods as possible rather than a narrow, restrictive diet.
3. Rotate food choices so that no undue emphasis is placed on the consumption of just a few foods over and over again.
4. Consume a raw salad with each meal and see to it that more than 50 percent of the food eaten is raw or semi-raw (steamed, stir-fried).
5. Think of foods in terms of basic staples and incidentals. The basic staples should be as close to nature as possible—a potato, an orange, a piece of chicken, etc. The incidentals or extras would be potato chips, orange soda, salami, etc. In the staple category, emphasize fresh vegetables, legumes, seeds and nuts, whole grains, and fruits and minimize foods of animal origin, such as meat, chicken, seafood, eggs and milk.

Nutrient supplementation can be an important element in recovery from CTS. Treatment with vitamin B6 has already been discussed. Although B6 in individualized dosage sufficient to normalize the condition and/or the EGOT test is the mainstay of nutrient supplementation, it must be recognized that all nutrients interact with one another. Hence a wide variety of nutrient supplements may be indicated. Nutrients to be considered in supplementation include all vitamins, nutrient minerals, amino acids, detoxifying herbs, diuretic herbs, healing and restorative herbs, etc. At all times, the advice of a competent nutritional professional should be followed.

GLANDULAR TTREATMENT

Laboratory tests are also of great value to determine the presence or absence of malfunction of the endocrine glands. Although many patients with CTS do *not* have glandular disorders, some do and these patients must be identified and properly treated.

Diabetes mellitus can be diagnosed and thyroid function assessed by laboratory tests. Unfortunately, some thyroid conditions are not discovered by merely measuring blood hormones. Broda Barnes, M.D. has pointed out that the basal body temperature (the armpit temperature taken first thing on arising) may give valuable information as an index of low thyroid function.[3] Current research by the Broda Barnes Foundation in Trumbull, Conn., utilizes a 24-hour urine collection to assess function of the thyroid and the adrenal glands. Also helpful is a blood level of the adrenal hormone DHEA.

The hormones of the gonads must also be considered because significant departures from normal may be encountered. Accordingly, estrogen, progesterone, and testosterone (free and total) may be assayed.

Of particular importance for therapeutic success is a view that encompasses the broad total of all glandular functions. One elderly patient of mine with bilateral CTS failed to find relief of pain and swelling in the hands and wrists until glandular-function tests revealed deficits of thyroid and adrenal hormones. Progressive improvement occurred with sequential treatment, first with natural thyroid, then natural adrenal hormones, and finally with natural testosterone.

Treatment of blood sugar, thyroid, adrenal, and gonadal disorders must be carried out with natural therapies whenever possible. For example, a program of nutritional therapy and programmed exercise may entirely do away with some cases of diabetes mellitus. Desiccated animal thyroid may be used instead of synthetic thyroid. Natural sources of adrenal hormones are available. Estrogen, progesterone, and testosterone from soybeans and yams are also available. At all times, medical supervision is required to assure that the natural therapies are appropriate and that proper doses are utilized to avoid undertreatment as well as overtreatment.

Physical Therapy

The physical therapist can provide a comprehensive program of help for most patients with CTS. He can perform soft tissue stretching and massage; he can provide electrical modalities such as ultrasound and interferential medium-frequency current to allay inflammation, splints to immobilize the wrist, and as noted previously, he may be able to invoke a functional analysis of the work situation. Sometimes, also, on the recommendation of the physician, he can administer corticosteroid medication by means of ionto-phoresis. In that technique, the corticosteroid anti-inflammatory medication is carried into the wrist tissues by means of gentle electric current. (The physician may also elect to inject corticosteroids into the carpal tunnel although that procedure carries the risk of injury to the median nerve.) Whenever imbalances or deficits of muscle strength are found, the physical therapist can also instruct the patient in appropriate remedial exercises.

The use of a splint to immobilize the wrist in order to rest the injured tissues may give excellent relief of symptoms. Because of the nocturnal worsening that so many patients experience, some patients elect to wear the splint at bedtime only. Others wear it even at work. Most often best results will eventuate by wearing a wrist splint with the wrist in the neutral position most of the time for several weeks at the onset of the disorder.

The availability of a convenient, lightweight splint such as the Carpal/Lock makes the wearing of a splint a comfort rather than a chore. According to Diane Hartley, R.P.T. of St. Petersburg, Fla., the Carpal/Lock splint is lightweight (2½ ounces), easily applicable, and readily removable because of its velcro straps. She notes that the splint holds the wrist in the neutral position without reducing dexterity. The Carpal/Lock splint is available from Meyer Distributing Company, P. O. Box 1150, Upland, CA 91785-1150.

NEUROMUSCULAR THERAPY

The use of neuromuscular therapy with the CTS patient involves the direct treatment of the soft tissues of the wrist as well as the treatment of the soft tissues of the remainder of the arm, shoulder girdle, neck, and trunk. Since human beings "hang together" it is rare to find people who do not have abnormally tight muscles or dysfunctional connective tissues (tendons, ligaments, fascia, or loose connective tissue) in areas apart from the affected wrist. Indeed, at times, the neuromuscular release of trigger points, tight muscles, or boggy muscles and connective tissues in the neck and trunk may serve as a vital catalyst for healing of tissues at the wrist. Neuromuscular therapy can be a potent force for health enhancement, including the eradication of CTS.

Neuromuscular therapy is far more specific and anatomically directed than the forms of massage known as Swedish, Esalen, Trager, etc. The latter are excellent tools for relaxation and improving the flow of blood and lymph throughout the muscular frame. In my experience, however, neuromuscular therapy for the hand, wrist, arm, shoulder girdle, neck, and trunk offers the most efficacious therapy of all the massage techniques.

The neuromuscular therapist, as recommended by Paul St. John, L.M.T. may also wish to utilize the poultice of burdock herb. Judith Walker, L.M.T. notes that the application of ice and cold (but beware frostbite), especially at bedtime, may be useful. Ms. Walker also indicates that alternation of heat and cold may be more helpful than cold alone.

MICROCURRENT ELECTRICAL STIMULATION

CTS may also be treated quite successfully by means of microcurrent electrical stimulation. Steve Stephenson and Dick Van Middlesworth, R.N., pain management specialists, use instruments known as the Acuscope and the Myopulse to engender micro-current up to 500 milliamperes. The Acuscope is more effective in promoting healing of nerves, and the Myopulse is more effective in calming inflammation or swelling of muscles, tendons, and ligaments.

The Acuscope is applied to both sides of the vertebrae from the first cervical to the fifth thoracic (since the median nerve originates from those segments of the spinal cord). The brachial plexus is then treated along with other median nerve points. Finally, local wrist points are treated. Bilateral treatment improves results.

The Myopulse is then applied to the wrist and adjacent areas as well as to any other tender areas including the forearm, shoulder, and neck.

If the condition is diagnosed early and treatment with micro-current is begun immediately, a few treatments usually enable the tissue to return to normal. If the precipitating movement activity which caused the condition must be continued (for example, a butcher who returns to his work), then follow-up treatments may be required as symptoms arise.

Spinal Manipulation

Spinal manipulation has been most effective in the management of pseudo-CTS that has its origin in cervical vertebral subluxations. However, it may also be a valid tool for the treatment of CTS itself. Sometimes my patients improve with spinal manipulation even though there is no known scientific reason for them to do so. Although subluxations of the vertebrae may be reduced, thus relieving pressure on pinched nerves, we do not know why spinal manipulation helps so many persons with CTS to feel better and function better.

On the other hand, if vertebral subluxations exist, and if they are putting pressure on the cervical spine nerve roots that form the median nerve, then a neuropathy of sorts may exist. That is, a pseudo-CTS may exist. Crouch and Madden present the hypothesis that such a condition may render the median nerve susceptible to injury by wrist compression.[4] In that view, the manipulative adjustment of cervical vertebrae to remove offending pressure on nerve roots would restore the nerve roots to health and eradicate the CTS. Although that mechanism may indeed occur, I suspect it is merely a contributory factor in most cases rather than a prime cause.

The use of therapeutic ultrasound or micro-current electrical stimulation applied to the wrist, arm, and neck may frequently be used by the supervising physician who will combine spinal manipulation with the electrical modalities. As with physical therapists and other physicians, the use of a wrist splint or splints along with an electrical modality can be a most effective approach employed by the manipulating physician. For the most part today, spinal manipulation is carried out by doctors of chiropractic, although some doctors of osteopathy and even fewer doctors of medicine may do so.

Acupuncture

As is the case with manipulative therapies, neuromuscular therapy, and micro-current electrical stimulation, the treatment of areas remote from the wrist may assist the median nerve to heal. Acupuncture, like long-distance running, induces the release of endorphins, the body's endogenous anti-pain chemicals.

John O'Neill, A.P. (acupuncture physician) of Clearwater, Fla., states that the connective tissue point is treated directly on the wrist crease as well as other points. Other measures such as vitamin B6, other nutrient supplements, and treatment of the sacral base are frequently employed. He believes—as do physical therapists, neuromuscular therapists, chiropractors, reflexologists, and nutritionists—that most patients do not require surgery for successful treatment of CTS.

Note, too, that the acupuncture points can also be treated by micro-current electrical stimulation as well as by acupressure.

REFLEXOLOGY

Dwight Byers is the "godfather" of reflexology.[5] Reflexology, a treatment modality that has been responsible for eradication of CTS in many patients, utilizes reflexes in the feet to alleviate conditions elsewhere in the body.

Ted Stansbery of the Harrison Wellness Clinic in Harrison, Ark., a former instructor of basic martial arts, a licensed massage therapist, and a certified reflexologist, has treated approximately a hundred individuals with CTS.[6] His primary tool of therapy is reflexology. Stansbery states that nearly all affected individuals have good results, and that those whose results are sub-standard are those who have had prior wounds that interfere with therapeutic progress.

How can one individual acquire the clinical experience that Stansbery has accumulated? Close to his treatment center are two businesses: Levi Strauss and the Cloud Corporation. The former fashions jeans, and the latter wood flooring. Levi Strauss uses sewing machines while the Cloud Corporation product is made by the use of rough-notch saws. The workers in these plants as well as the secretaries who work at computers make up the clients that Stansbery treats.

Prior to the utilization of Stansbery's therapy, the industrial companies had been sending their employees with CTS to Fayetteville for surgery. The expense to the companies was $2500.00 for surgery (on one hand) in addition to the time lost from work (nine weeks for one hand and longer for two) and the cost of medications. In addition, the affected employees not infrequently required second or third operations.

Stansbery's treatment consists of extensive reflexology. The patient comes for one-hour treatments twice weekly during work hours. He treats the feet primarily but also the hands and arms and the *teres major* and *minor* muscles. Stansbery has made the observation that nearly every patient has been found to have an extremely sensitive spot just above the elbow on the inner side of the arm. He states, "I work this area and its referral in the leg in a proximal motion." He notes that "this sensitivity will decrease greatly as you work with it." The younger the client and the more recent the symptoms, the more quickly the patient recovers. In the absence of other complications (torn muscles, old scar tissue, etc.), the patient recovers in approximately two months and may return to his previous job.

HOMEOPATHY

I do not see homeopathy as a potent tool for alleviation of most cases of CTS, but I do recognize the power of therapeutic belief that can be responsible for miraculous benefits. Those who elect to utilize homeopathy as the principal therapy must seek supervision or continuing counsel from an objective observer. Homeopathic treatment that tunes into one's energy channels may eradicate symptoms, but one must be certain that manual function by objective assessment is normal and that muscle wasting does not develop.

I have never seen any serious side effects from homeopathic treatments. In fact, homeopathy can be a valuable adjunct to other management measures. Some topical homeopathic preparations that may be applied to the palm and wrist are Traumeel and Zeel homeopathic ointments.

NUTRITIONAL MEDICINE

As previously stated, the nutritional measures that are likely to be important in the management of CTS include vitamin B6 therapy and other supportive B vitamins, optimalization of the diet, and a wide variety of other nutrient supplements, preferably customized for individual needs. In this section, I intend to present and discuss other therapeutic maneuvers available to the physician whose focus lies primarily in the nutritional area.

Much symptomatic relief can be obtained by the use of natural measures to counter inflammation and swelling. Bromelain, an extract from the pineapple, can be very effective when used orally in high doses on an empty stomach. The bioflavonoid quercetin is also an effective anti-inflammatory agent. Particularly helpful have been protease concentrate or traumagesic capsules (Plant Enzyme Therapy, Tyler Encapsulations, Gresham, OR) or proteolytic enzymes (Miller Pharmacal Group, Inc., West Chicago, IL.) I place most of my patients on the multiple vitamin Theramill Forte (also made by Miller Pharmacal Group, Inc.) When taken in the recommended dose, Theramill Forte provides 100 mg of B6 as pyridoxine hydrochloride, 25 mg as pyridoxal-5-phosphate, 400 units of vitamin E, with many other nutrients also in good supply. Protease, traumagesic, and proteolytic enzymes are best taken on an empty stomach to enhance absorption. Theramill Forte should be taken with meals. Undoubtedly, there are many other suitable preparations.

Adverse side effects from these nutrients or others like them are very infrequent. Thus, for most persons, most useful natural nutrients may replace medications in combatting swelling, pain, and limitation of function. At all times, the counsel of a competent nutritional counselor must be followed.

Burdock may be used orally as well as topically for its anti-inflammatory action. The spice-derivative curcumin may also be taken orally. The proteolytic enzyme chymotrypsin, taken on an empty stomach, is effective. Ginger by mouth as well as topically by compress may alleviate inflammation.

Conventional physicians confronted with CTS patients are likely to prescribe nonsteroidal anti-inflammatory drugs (NSAIDs) of which there are a large number (acetylsalicylic acid or aspirin, ibuprofen or Motrin, indomethacin or Indocin, naproxen or Naprosyn, tolmetin or Tolectin, sulindac or Clinoril, and others). Those drugs constitute the tools that physicians are taught to use in order to suppress inflammation that causes pain and interference with function. Indeed, those NSAIDs are effective. The only question is: At what price? Many persons have gastrointestinal side effects. One patient of mine came to me after the use of an NSAID that resulted in severe gastrointestinal hemorrhage requiring surgery and lifesaving transfusions. Others develop chronic gastritis or ulcers. The risk is so extensive that many physicians who use NSAIDs place their patients on other strong drugs to block the excretion of gastric hydrochloric acid. Not surprisingly, *those* drugs have their own set of unwanted side effects. Be aware that there is a significant likelihood of rebound inflammation when the drugs are discontinued. Then, too, there is scientific evidence that indicates that NSAIDs themselves actually produce a degeneration of connective tissue in the body.[7,8,9,10,11] Finally, one must cope with the fact that most, if not all, NSAIDs contain unwanted binders, fillers, sugars, dyes, colors, or flavors, adding to the body's burden of xenobiotics (foreign chemicals) which can further impede tissue repair.

I do not wish to suggest that there is no place for the use of NSAIDs. Some people who do not respond to more natural forms of anti-inflammatory treatment or who do not desire to use the more natural therapies may, indeed, require their use. Then, too, short-term use might be appropriate for some persons who have not sufficiently informed themselves of available alternatives. Nevertheless, natural therapy is always preferred when it is sufficient to provide relief.

The natural approach to the treatment of CTS will also call for replacement of the birth control pill, whenever it is used, with other forms of pregnancy prevention. Whenever "the pill" is being used to regulate or improve the menstrual cycle and the menstrual periods, more natural hormones will usually suffice.

The birth control pill has as its ingredients synthetic estrogens and progestins that effectively prevent pregnancy but are thought to lack the desirable effects of their natural counterparts. Moreover, the various side effects of "the pill" such as Candida yeast overgrowth and nutrient deficiencies must be considered.

If "the pill" has been used to manage painful periods, premenstrual or postmenstrual disorders, irregular periods or the like, then attempts must be made to find a nutritional approach to enhance the patient's well-being and to improve the menstrual state. A host of management measures can be invoked. Diet must be surveyed and improved. Vitamin A blood level measurements will often disclose lower-than-desirable levels. Vitamins A, B6, pantothenic acid, B complex, vitamins C and E, magnesium, zinc, essential fatty acids, and other nutrients may effectively transform the patient into a happy, well-adjusted individual who sails through her cycles with minimal or no complaints. Needed at all times, of course, is a professional nutritional counselor.

The fact remains that in some cases the natural, nutritional approach to menstrual disorders may not suffice to provide the degree of improvement available by use of hormone therapy. For those cases, there are excellent preparations of micronized estrogens and progesterone from natural sources (soybean and yam). Their availability in capsules free of dyes, colors, flavors, binders, and fillers or as gels that are applied to the skin permits a truly effective natural treatment of female cyclic and menstrual disorders. I must, however, caution that the use of natural estrogens and progesterone at this time *cannot* be relied upon for the prevention of pregnancy.

Although conventional medical views often indicate that food allergies are much rarer than usually believed, I find that food intolerances, food sensitivities, food toxicities, or food reactions of one kind or another are very commonly implicated in the origin of a wide variety of dysfunctions in the body. A most common manifestation of those food reactions is swelling (edema or water retention). That swelling can be thought of as nature's attempt to dilute the offending food.

Since the swelling of tissues in the cramped carpal tunnel is a major component of most cases of median nerve dysfunction, the alleviation of any edematous state can be helpful or curative in CTS. Identification and alleviation of food (and chemical) reactions, thus, may be crucial in the management of CTS.

Certain individuals have adverse reactions to the nightshade foods: tomatoes, potatoes, eggplant, and bell peppers. I know of no scientific test to indicate the presence or absence of nightshade sensitivity other than elimination of those foods (for a period of three months or more) and subsequent reintroduction/challenge.

Other substances that commonly cause unwanted reactions may include milk and milk products, wheat, yeast, eggs, citrus, chocolate, soy, and chemicals in foods or medications. One may choose to eliminate those foods one at a time, or undergo a fast for four days followed by individual food challenges. Or, one can consume an "elemental diet" using Vivonex for one to three weeks followed by individual food challenges. All of these approaches must be done with the careful guidance of a competent nutritional supervisor.

One of the easiest and most successful treatments is to detoxify the body by means of an appropriate herbal program as well as ridding the body of all simple sugars and excess salt. A competent nutritional counselor can supply the details of herbal detoxification programs.

I find the 21-day "detox" program of Titrex herbs from Titrex

International, U.S.A., most effective and quite safe. The herbs useful in countering inflammation and pain are devil's claw, meadowsweet, and black currant. In some cases, the doses of particular herbs may need to be quite high. A synergistic combination proven effective for swelling consists of artichoke, Java tea, dandelion, horsetail, and meadowsweet. If the problem is primarily arthritis, the synergistic combination is black currant, devil's claw, horsetail, and meadowsweet.

Simple sugars can be eradicated by not consuming sugar in all of its multiple forms.[12] Sometimes even fruit juices and fruits must be avoided. Sugar is an osmotically active substance that holds water in the body, as does salt. Therefore, ridding the body of unneeded sugar and excess salt can significantly decrease the edema of the tissues in the carpal tunnel area. The use of herbal diuretics may also be helpful in decompressing swollen tissues that unduly crowd the median nerve in the carpal tunnel. Never, however, must they replace competent professional management.

At times, a course of colonic irrigations may be invoked as a means of detoxification. For those who require it, most satisfactory results are seen. I suspect that colonic irrigations may be effective by eliminating toxic reactions in the body that produce edema in vulnerable tissues such as the overworked wrist.

SURGERY

Many patients will consult a medical doctor in regard to their symptoms of CTS. It is the physician's responsibility to identify or confirm the diagnosis and to find the most appropriate therapy for the condition and for the particular patient who has the condition. The physician's task is to accurately sift out the "wheat" from the "chaff" in order to address issues that are significant to the patient and that bear upon his condition.

The general physician may elect to become involved in the patient's job factors, he may wish to recommend the use of a splint, he may suggest the use of vitamin B6 up to 100 or 200 mg per day for a period of three months (accompanied by a multivitamin), and he may counsel the patient as to the use of anti-inflammatory drugs. At other times, he may refer the patient to a physical therapist or to a neuromuscular therapist. Often, however, he will refer the patient directly to a general surgeon, an orthopedic surgeon, a plastic surgeon, or a neurosurgeon for definitive care. Although the surgeon may elect to carry out all those same treatments, the likelihood is that the surgeon will use surgery, the tool of his trade, in order to resolve the CTS.

There is no question that surgery, properly done, will usually result in prompt clearing of all symptoms with minimal, if any, side effects. The question is, however, does one really wish to submit to "the knife" in order to clear up a disorder that may respond nicely to nonsurgical measures? In other words, should surgery be done early in the game or reserved for those few patients who fail to respond to the nonsurgical measures? For those who come to therapeutic attention late with chronic numbness in the fingers and atrophy of the thumb muscles, prompt surgical attention, along with all other supportive and rehabilitative measures, is required. Prognostication of outcome grows increasingly uncertain the longer the condition has been present.

I have a number of patients who elected to have early surgery and who have had complete remission of all symptoms without any unwanted side effects. I have others who had mediocre results. The surgeons state that it is the most successful and gratifying surgery that they perform. They indicate excellent results in 90 to 95 percent of their cases. There is no question, however, that some surgical patients do well for one to two years only to have a relapse of CTS in the hand operated on, presumably because of fibrosis, scarring, or progression of inflammation that impinge upon the median nerve in the carpal tunnel.

Although the percentage of patients who don't improve at all with surgery is quite small, for the specific individual concerned that failure percentage is 100 percent. One reason for failure is incomplete transection of the *two* bands of the transverse carpal ligament. More often, however, the patient has pseudo-CTS. In those cases, the physical therapist or neuromuscular therapist is usually called upon to evaluate and treat the patient. Judith Walker, L.M.T., states that the surgical failures that she sees for neuromuscular therapy are nearly always those whose wrist and hand symptoms arise from hypertonic muscles, entrapment of nerve, and trigger points in the arm, shoulder, and neck.

When considering surgery, one must be concerned about the risk of anesthesia, the possibility of surgical error, the possible need for blood transfusions with their attendant risks, and the long healing time. With CTS, however, the anesthesia is usually local rather than general, the surgeons who perform the surgery are usually well-versed in their surgical craft, blood transfusions are almost never needed, and recovery time for the patient is usually only a few days to a week or two. Speaking for surgery too is the prompt, definitive nature of the surgery (the entire transverse carpal ligament is transected) with its rapid relief of symptoms, the relatively small scar, and the availability of endoscopic surgery to transect the ligament. Troublesome aftereffects are few although it is possible for the patient to develop reflex sympathetic dystrophy in which pain, numbness, and parasthesias persist and may worsen.

The decision whether or not to have surgery ultimately comes down to the orientation and awareness of the patient. If the patient is mechanistically inclined in his thinking, he will more often gravitate to a surgical procedure. If the patient is more open to alternative medicine, he is likely to choose the nonsurgical approach. Often a choice of treatment is made on the basis of the experience of one's friends. If Susie and Mark had good results with surgery performed by Dr. X, then the symptomatic patient may tilt in that direction. For many individuals, the cost factor and the availability of insurance to pay for a work-related disorder will figure prominently in their decision about surgical treatment. And some people will elect to have surgery because it offers a quick solution to the condition.

In uncomplicated cases of CTS of recent onset, I urge initial, conservative, natural therapies. I reserve surgery for those patients who fail to respond to the procedures discussed in this book. At any time, however, if symptoms worsen, I would quickly invoke the services of a surgeon. It is foolish to blindly persist in natural therapies that fail to improve the condition. Delay in relieving the pressure on the median nerve can lead to lasting loss of function.

CONCLUSION

In many respects, CTS, like chronic fatigue syndrome, is the "in" disease of our times. In years gone by, it was neurasthenia, hysteria, minimal brain dysfunction, and hypoglycemia. All of these were or are conditions that go along with certain historical periods. Some authors have suggested that some diseases are inextricably linked with the cultures in which they exist. The notion is that the disorders are at least as much a product of the cultural values, styles, language, and thought as they are of germs and famine and natural catastrophes.

Had we not an industrial revolution, CTS would probably have remained an obscure disorder limited to a few individuals who were pregnant, diabetic, hypothyroid, or relegated to chopping stakes for the erection of tents. Machines, factories, keyboards and all the other accoutrements of industrial society are now a *fait accompli*. And along with them we have inherited white bread, candy, soda, chips, donuts, sugar, pies, hot dogs and the host of processed-refined-chemicalized convenience items that displace from our dinner plates the kale, asparagus, sweet potatoes, cabbage, black beans, steel-cut oatmeal, fruits, brown rice, and romaine upon which our health depends. The combination of the repetitive mechanical tasks of our culture with the sedentary or near-sedentary nature of the jobs that generate those tasks along with the subnutritive and monotonous diets that are so common today brings to our era a number of health problems, one of which is carpal tunnel syndrome.

I suggest that anyone who has the symptoms of CTS read and reread this text. Discuss the issue with others. Obtain the judgment of your physician. Then go off somewhere under a tree to settle the issues in your mind and proceed to the treatment that feels right for you. The likelihood is that you will be successful, whatever you choose, if the therapist rendering the treatment is knowledgeable, experienced, careful, and honest enough to refer you for alternative treatments when and if his is not getting good results. With that mind-set and the awareness that this book has engendered within you, you have a good chance of overcoming Carpal Tunnel Syndrome without surgery.

REFERENCES

ANATOMY

1. Cailliet, Rene, M.D. *Hand Pain and Impairment*. Philadelphia: F. A. Davis Co., 1982.

2. Cailliet, Rene, M.D. *Soft Tissue Pain and Disability*. 2nd Ed. Philadelphia: F. A. Davis Co., 1988.

3. Crouch, Tammy, and Madden, Michael, D.C. *Carpal Tunnel Syndrome & Overuse Injuries, Prevention, Treatment & Recovery*. Berkeley, CA: North Atlantic Books, 1992.

4. Runge, Val M., Ed. *Clinical Magnetic Resonance Imaging*. Philadelphia: J. B. Lippincott Co., 1990.

SYMPTOMS

1. Cailliet, Rene, M.D. *Hand Pain and Impairment*. Philadelphia: F. A. Davis Co., 1982.

THE ELLIS FUNCTIONAL TEST

1. Werbach, Melvyn R., *Nutritional Influences on Illness. A Sourcebook of Clinical Research*. New Canaan, CT: Keats Publishing, Inc., p. 123, 1990.

CAUSATIVE FACTORS

1. Cailliet, Rene, M.D. *Hand Pain and Impairment*. Philadelphia: F. A. Davis Co., 1982.

2. "Musicians Who Play Too Much Risk Painful Injury," St. Petersburg, *Florida Times*, February 19, 1989.

3. Lederman, Richard, M.D. "An Overview of Performing Arts Medicine," *The American Music Teacher*, February/March 1991, pp. 12–15 and 70–71.

4. *Taber's Cyclopedia Medical Dictionary*, 6th ed. no date or publisher given, quoted by Nimmo, Raymond L., D. C. in Receptor-Tonus Technique, unpublished paper, undated, supplied by Judith Walker, L.M.T.

5. Cailliet, Rene, M.D. *Soft Tissue Pain and Disability*. 2nd Ed. Philadelphia: F. A. Davis Co., 1988.

6. Hebert, Lauren A., P.T. *Living with C.T.D.* Bangor, ME: IMPACC, 1990.

CTS as Vitamin B6 Deficiency

1. Ellis, J. M., Kishi, T., Azuma, J., and Folkers, K. *Res. Commun. Chem. Path. Pharmacol.* 13, No. 4: 743–757, 1976.

2. Ellis, J. M., Azuma, J., Watanake, T., Folkers, K., Lowel, J., Hurst, G. A., Ahn, C. H., Shuford, E., Jr., and Ulrich, R. F. *Res. Commun. Chem. Path. Pharmacol.* 17, 165–178, 1977.

3. Folkers, Karl, Ellis, John, Watanabe, Tatsuo, Saji, Seizuke, and Kaji, Masahiro. "Biochemical Evidence for a Deficiency of Vitamin B6 in the Carpal Tunnel Syndrome Based on a Crossover Clinical Study," *Proc. Natl. Acad. Sci.*, USA 75 (7): 3410–12, July 1978.

4. Ellis, John M. *et al.* "Response of vitamin B6 deficiency and the carpal tunnel syndrome to pyridoxine," *Proc. Natl. Acad. Sci.*, USA, 79: 7494–98, 1982.

5. Smith, G., Rudge, P. and Peters, T. "Biochemical Studies of Pyridoxal and Pyridoxal Phosphate Status and Therapeutic Trial of Pyridoxine in Patients with Carpal Tunnel Syndrome," *Ann. Neurol.* 15: 194–107, 1984.

6. Beyers, C., Delisa, J., Frankel, D., and Kraft, G. "Pyridoxine Metabolism in Carpal Tunnel Syndrome With and Without Peripheral Neuropathy," *Arch. Phys. Med. Rehabil.*, 65 (11): 712–16, 1984.

7. Bernstein, Allan L., M.D., and Dinesen, Jamie S., R.N. "Brief Communication: Effect of Pharmacologic Doses of Vitamin B6 on Carpal Tunnel Syndrome, Electroencephalographic Results, and Pain," *Journal of the American College of Nutrition*, 12 (1): 73–76, 1993.

8. Parry, G. J. and Bredesen, D. E. "Sensory Neuropathy with Low-dose Pyridoxine," *Neurology* 35: 1466–68, 1985.

9. Schaumburg, H. H., Berger, A. "Pyridoxine Neurotoxicity," in Leklem, J. E., Reynolds, R. D. (eds): *Clinical and Physiological Applications of Vitamin B6*. New York: Alan Liss, Inc., pp. 402–413, 1988.

10. Yoshida, I., Sakaguchi, Y., Nakano, M., *el al.* "Pyridoxal Phosphate-induced Liver Injury in a Patient with Homocystinuria," *J. Inherit. Metab. Dis.* 8: 91, 1985.

11. Parry, G. J., and Bredesen, D. E. "Sensory Neuropathy with Low-dose Pyridoxine," *Neurology* 35: 1466–68, 1985.

12. Folkers, Carl, Ph.D., D.Sc. (x2), M.D. (honorary), personal communication, January 11, 1993.

Functional Enzyme Test of B6

1. Wright, Jonathan V., M.D. *Dr. Wright's Guide to Healing with Nutrition*, New Canaan, CT: Keats Publishing, Inc., pp. 522–530, 1984.

2. Folkers, Karl, Ellis, John, Watanabe, Tatsuo, Saji, Seizuke, and Kaji, Masahiro. "Biochemical Evidence for a Deficiency of Vitamin B6 in the Carpal Tunnel Syndrome Based on a Crossover Clinical Study," *Proc. Natl. Acad. Sci.*, USA 75 (7): 3410–12, July 1978.

3. Smith, Gillian P., Ph.D., Rudge, P. J., FRCP, and Peters, T. J. "Biochemical Studies of Pyridoxal and Pyridoxal Phosphate Status and Therapeutic Trial of Pyridoxine in Patients with Carpal Tunnel Syndrome," *Annals of Neurology*, Vol. 15, No. 1, pp. 104–7, January 1984.

4. Pangborn, Jon, personal communication, February 10th, 1993.

5. St. John, Paul, personal communication, December 28, 1992.

TREATMENT

1. Diane Hartley, R.P.T., personal communication, December 22, 1992.

2. Hebert, Lauren A., P.T. *Living with C.T.D.* Bangor, ME: IMPACC, 1990.

3. Barnes, Broda, M.D., and Galton, Lawrence. *The Unsuspected Illness.* N.Y.: Harper and Row, Publishers, 1976.

4. Crouch, Tammy, and Madden, Michael, D.C. *Carpal Tunnel Syndrome & Overuse Injuries, Prevention, Treatment, & Recovery.* Berkeley, CA: North Atlantic Books, 1992.

5. Byers, Dwight, *Better Health With Foot Reflexology,* St. Petersburg, FL: Ingham Publishing, 1983.

6. Stansbery, Ted, personal communication, February 3rd, 1993.

7. Brooks, P. M., Potter, S. R., and Buchanan, W. W. "NSAID and Osteoarthritis—Help or Hindrance," *J. Rheumatol.,* 9: pp. 3–5, 1982.

8. Newman, N. M., and Ling, R. S. M. "Acetabular Bond Destruction Related to Non-steroidal Anti-inflammatory Drugs," *Lancet,* ii: pp. 11–13, 1985.

9. Solomon L. "Drug Induced Arthropathy and Necrosis of the Femoral Head," *J. Bone Joint Surg.,* 55B: pp. 246–251, 1973.

10. Ronningen, H. and Langeland, N. "Indomethacin Treatment in Osteoarthritis of the Hip Joint," *Acta Scand.,* 50: pp. 169–174, 1979.

11. Dequeker, J., Burssens, A., and Bouillon, R. "Dynamics of Growth Hormone Secretion in Patients with Osteoporosis and in Patients with Osteoarthrosis," *Hormone Res.,* 16: pp. 353–356, 1982.

12. Wunderlich, Ray C., Jr., M.D. *Sugar and Your Health,* St. Petersburg, FL: Good Health Publications, Johnny Reads, Inc., 1982.